God and Moses Led

Written by Jennifer Holder
Illustrated by Nancy Munger

Based on Exodus 3–40; Deuteronomy 31–34

God Said and Moses Led copyright © 2012 by Tyndale House Publishers, Inc., Carol Stream, Illinois 60188. All rights reserved. www.tyndale.com/kids. Originally published by Standard Publishing, Cincinnati, Ohio. First printing by Tyndale House Publishers, Inc., in 2016. Design: Sandra Wimmer. *TYNDALE*, Tyndale's quill logo, and *Happy Day* are registered trademarks of Tyndale House Publishers, Inc. For manufacturing information regarding this product, please call 1-800-323-9400.

ISBN 978-1-4143-9483-1

Printed in the United States of America

22	21	20	19	18	17
7	6	5	4	3	2

Tyndale House Publishers, Inc.
Carol Stream, Illinois

God called to Moses from a burning bush in the desert. God had heard the cries of his people who were slaves under Pharaoh. God chose Moses to lead his people out of slavery and out of Egypt.

But Moses was worried and afraid.
He asked, "Who am I to be the leader?"

God said, "I will be with you."

God said, "Tell Pharaoh to let my people go."

Moses and his brother Aaron went to Pharaoh's court. Moses delivered God's message to Pharaoh, but Pharaoh did not want to let go of his slaves.

God said, "Pharaoh will not listen to you, so I will show my great power."

Moses used God's power to perform amazing signs. God turned Moses' wooden staff into a snake. He turned the Nile River to blood. He called terrible plagues down on Egypt.

Finally, Pharaoh listened.

Moses led the people out. But soon, Pharaoh decided to chase them and bring them back as slaves again! What were Moses and God's people going to do?

God said, "Raise your hand over the sea."

Moses raised his hand. The sea's water parted!
God made a path for the people to cross over.

All of God's people crossed on dry ground. As soon as the Egyptians tried to follow, the water came crashing in on them.

Moses led the people away from the sea. They camped in the wilderness, but they didn't find any water. The people asked Moses, "What will we drink?" God answered by making bitter water into good water.

The people complained again. They asked, "What will we eat?" God gave them quail to eat in the evening. In the morning, God gave them bread called manna.

God said, "I will give you all you need every day."

God said, "You have seen all the amazing things I have done to rescue you from Egypt." He asked, "Will you agree to obey me and be my special people?"

The people answered, "We will do what God commands."

Moses went up on a mountain covered by a thick cloud. Thunder rumbled over it and lightning flashed. God told Moses the commands his people should follow.

Moses helped the people do what God said. They set up a beautiful place to worship God. They brought offerings and gifts to honor him.

Moses led God's people for 40 years. He appointed other wise leaders to help him. He led the fighting men in battles against their enemies. Then he taught Joshua to be the next leader of God's people.

Moses led God's people right to the edge of the good land that God had promised to give them.

Moses said, "Always remember what God did for you. If you obey his commands, he will bless you."